FAIL
NATION

FAIL NATION

A Visual Romp Through the World of Epic Fails

failblog.org

HARPER

NEW YORK · LONDON · TORONTO · SYDNEY

HARPER

HarperCollins books may be purchased for educational, business, or sales promotional use. For information please write: Special Markets Department, HarperCollins Publishers, 10 East 53rd Street, New York, NY 10022.

Writing, editing: Sonya Vatomsky and Ben Huh
Map and icon design: Joe Rufa

Designed by Emily Cavett Taff

Library of Congress Cataloging-in-Publication Data is available upon request.

ISBN 978-0-06-183399-1

11 12 13 QGT 10 9 8

To all the failers out there,
we pour this forty in your honor.

_____ was here **FIRST!**

FIRST!!.!!

No your not.

You spelt "youre" wrong

You SPELLED "spelt" right, but spelt in a hexaploid species of wheat.

𝄢 𝄢 𝄢 𝄢 𝄢

CONTENTS

Contents

♔ ♔ ♔ ♔ ♔

YOUR FAILPLANE HAS LANDED.

Welcome to FAIL Nation!

Long overlooked by vacationers, the small landlocked country of FAIL Nation has recently enjoyed a 9,000 percent increase in tourism after a certain dilettante proclaimed its coastline "the most beautiful in the world."

This book explores the majestic sights and sounds of FAIL Nation and provides thoughtful lodging recommendations for those on a budget of less than $3 a week as well as activity suggestions for those traveling with children, cripples, or crippled children.

We hope you enjoy your stay.

— The FAIL Nation Bureau of Tourism,
in partnership with the FAIL Nation
Bureau of Criminals

FAIL Nation Facts
current as of 1928

Population: *You*

Capital: *Moved from Brownsburg to FAIL City in 2005*

Area: *Slightly less than 5 times the size of Quebec*

Economy: *Failing*

National Flower: *The Faceplant*

National Language: *English as a Second Language (ESL)*

National Anthem: *"Never Gonna Give You Up" by Rick Astley (Brit., b. 1966)*

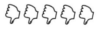

GETTING STARTED

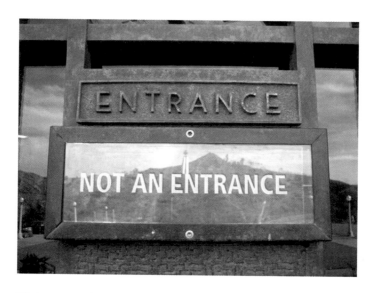

Welcome to FAIL Nation. Please enter (if you can).

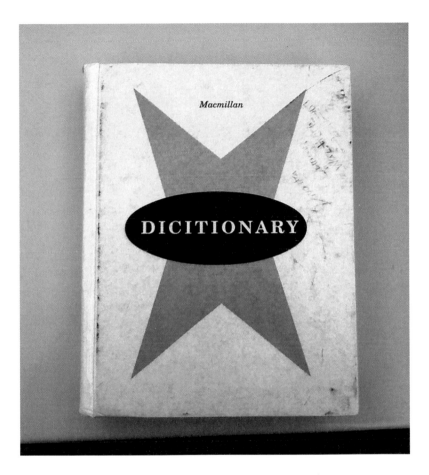

A dictionary will help you communicate with the natives.

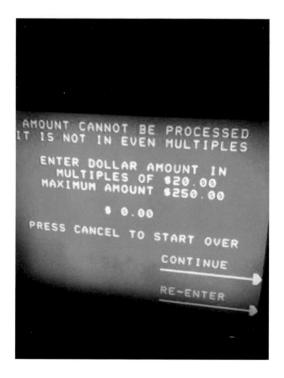

Convert your cash to Fail Dollars, or use one of our ATMs to withdraw money in the local currency. We recommend that you withdraw the maximum.

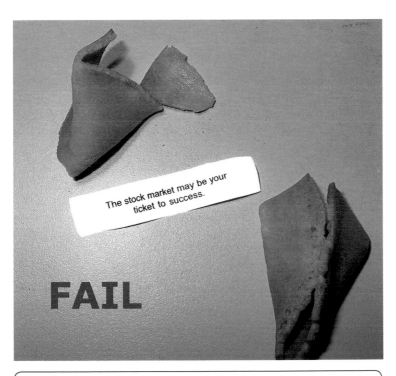

The stock market may be your ticket to success.

FAIL

ProTip: Take some of that cash and put it in the stock market.

Know where to find information about prevalent diseases and common toxic substances.

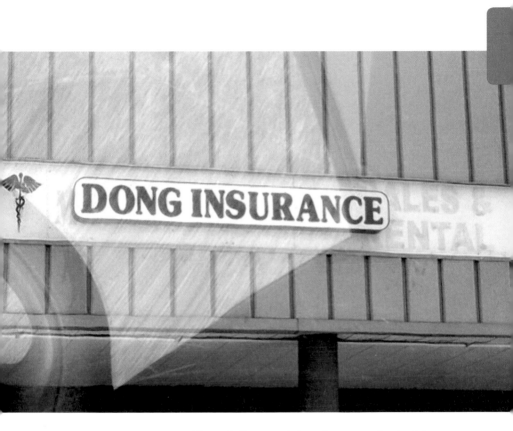

Insure your valuables. Especially your *ahem* personal valuables.

Re: General Manager
Marie Hosentroph <marie.hosentroph@marriott.com> 🖼 Add   To: ▓▓▓▓▓▓▓▓▓▓

Dear Mr Bell,

Thank you for your e-mail requesting the name of our General Manager, but unfortunately unless a valid reason is given we will not be divulging this information to you and have requested that my colleagues do the same.

Yours Sincerely,
Marie Hosentroph

Marie Hosentroph
P.A. to General Manager (Martin Cron)
Marriott Bristol Royal Hotel
College Green, Bristol, BS1 5TA

FAIL

Direct tel: 0117 9 105307
Hotel tel: 0117 9 255100 extension 6001
Direct fax: 0117 9 304740

This communication contains information from Marriott International, Inc. that may be confidential. sender, any person who receives this information is prohibited from disclosing, copying, distributing immediately delete it and all copies, and promptly notify the sender. Nothing in this communication

If you haven't already made hotel reservations, see our chapter on lodgings.

Note: Names have been changed to protect the failers.

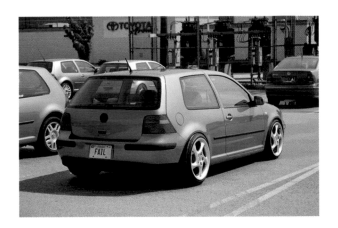

Rent a car and start your journey.

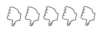

What is the nature of your visit to FAIL Nation?

(A) Visiting colleges

(B) Fleeing from law

(C) Anniversary

(C) Other _____

(please explain)

*If you picked (C) Fleeing from law, would you like a brochure from the FAIL Nation Bureau of Criminals? [Y] [N]

How much money would you like to spend?

(A) Less than $50

(B) Less than $55

(C) Money is not a concern

Are you traveling with children?

(A) Yes

(B) No

(C) Not yet

If you answered mostly (A): the Budget tour is right for you.

If you answered mostly (B): the Active Lifestyle tour will best meet your needs.

If you answered mostly (C): make enough memories to last a whole lifetime with the Romantic tour.

WHAT
TO DO

- - - - - - - - - - - - - - - -

PACKAGED TOURS

The FAIL Nation Bureau of Tourism offers several day-trips to accommodate the needs and budgets of all of our visitors, ranging from expensive to incredibly overpriced.

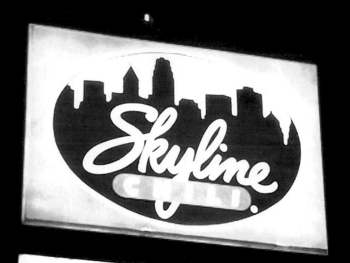

DRIVE THRU

MOM SAYS
TREAT DAD
TO A 3 WAY

DAY-TRIP 1: *Romantic*

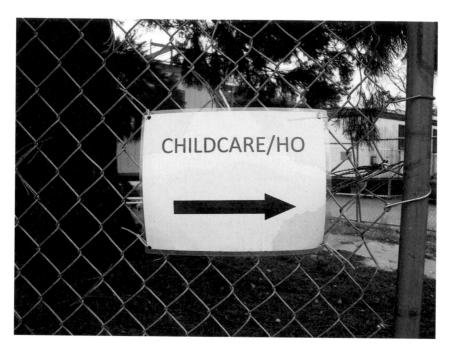

If you brought your children to FAIL Nation, enjoy complimentary day-care service while you see the sights. Our child-care workers are highly experienced in the art of child-rearing.

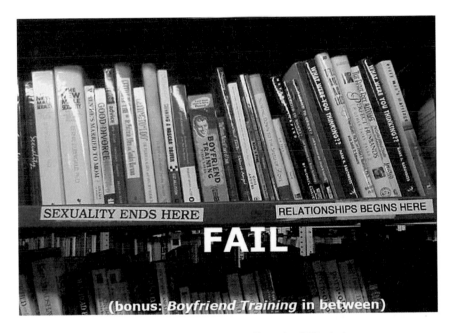

Learn more about your partner at our Couples' Workshop, provided by the FAIL Nation Library. We support our Library's!

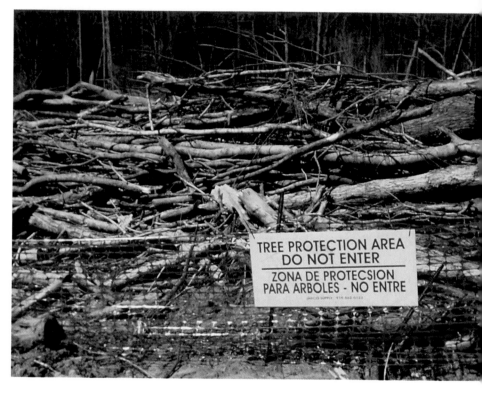

Why not have a picnic in our beautiful Tree Protection Area?

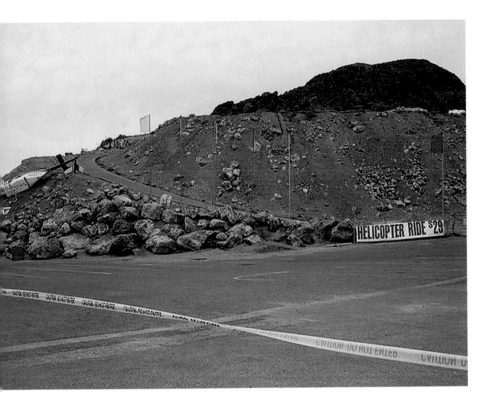

Show off your wild side with a helicopter ride for two. Our Pilot's License course takes only fifteen minutes.

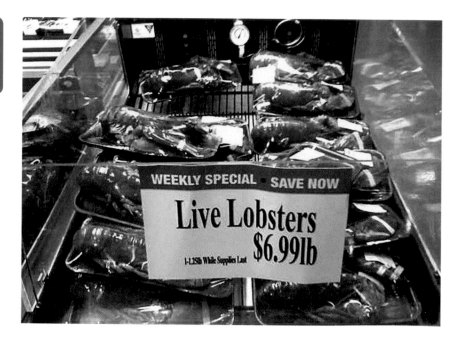

Treat your loved one to a live lobster dinner.

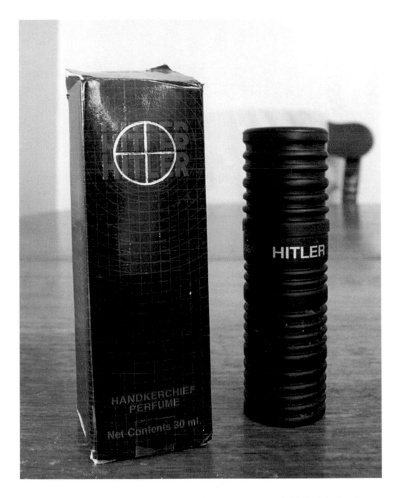

Head back to your hotel with a free sample of FAIL Nation's most romantic perfume.

ECONOMY
INN
GOD BLESS
AMERICA
FREE CUNT
BREAKFAST

👎👎👎👎👎

DAY-TRIP 2:
Budget

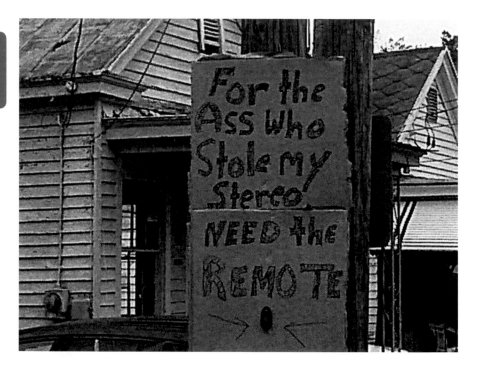

Certain neighborhoods offer great budget shopping deals.

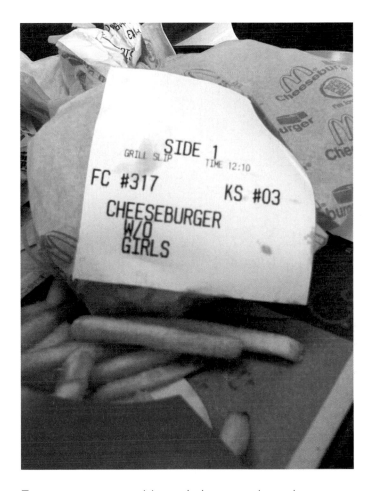

To save money, consider ordering your cheeseburger without girls. They cost extra.

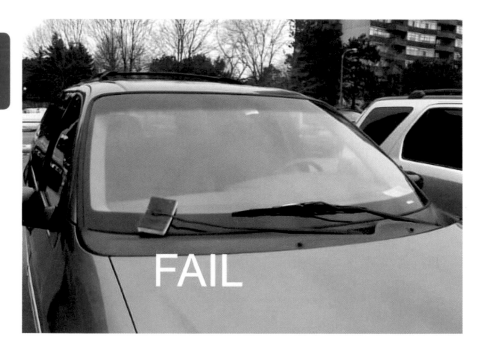

Rent a car from a local instead of an agency.

Know where to find free parking, but beware of restrictions.

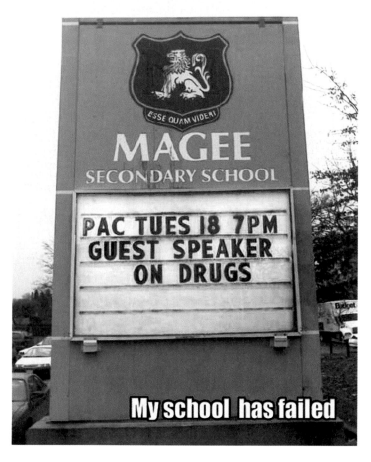

Be on the lookout for unusual free entertainment, such as public speakers at schools or churches.

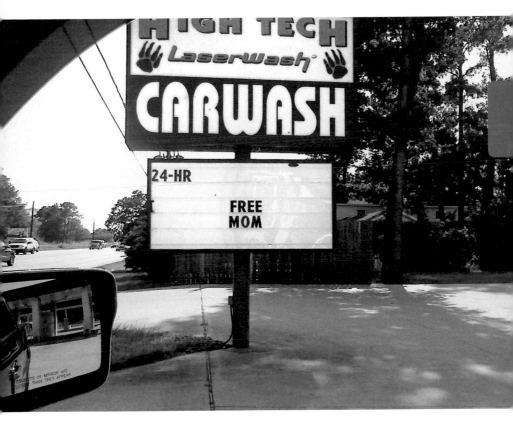

In 2008, FAIL Nation reported a surplus in moms. To celebrate, many small businesses are now giving them away for free.

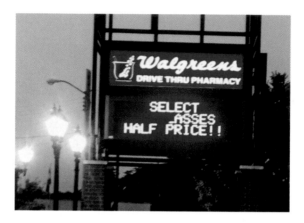

Know where to get good deals on spare parts.
You never know when you might need them!

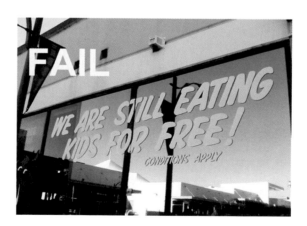

Some deals should be avoided.

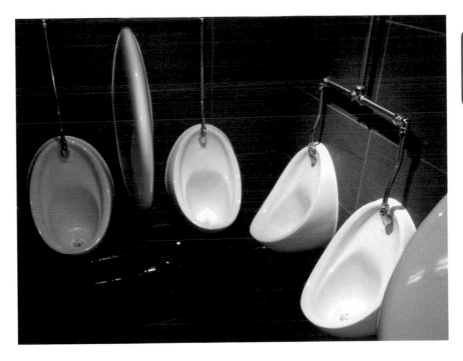

Save on lodging by opting for a shared bathroom.

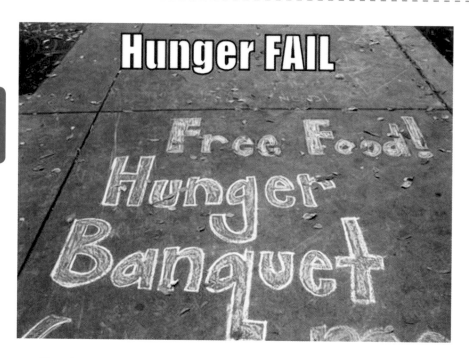

Find free food at the neighborhood Hunger Banquets, which occur monthly in the fall in honor of FAIL Nation's legendary less-than-bountiful harvest season.

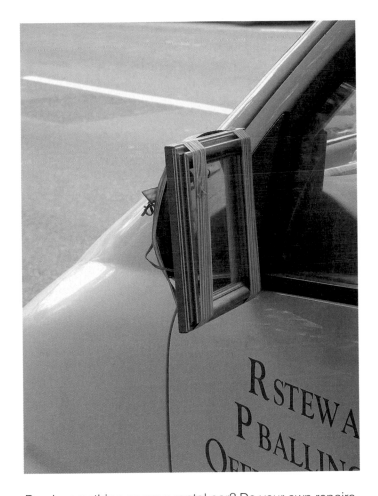

Break something on your rental car? Do your own repairs, like this FAIL native.

DAY-TRIP 3:
Active Lifestyle

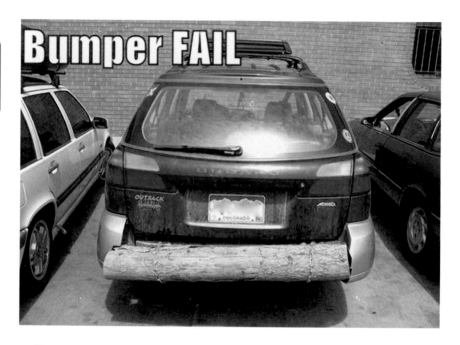

Rent a car suited to your adventurous needs.

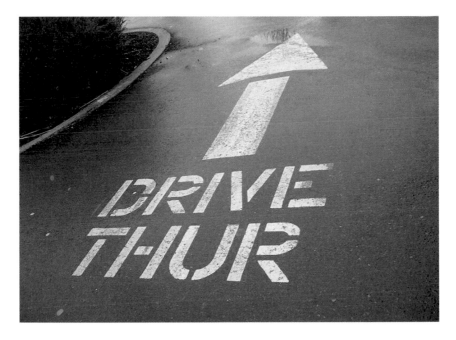

Experience the active life without all the walking and jogging! Many of FAIL Nation's attractions have a car-based option for the hyper of mind and lazy of body.

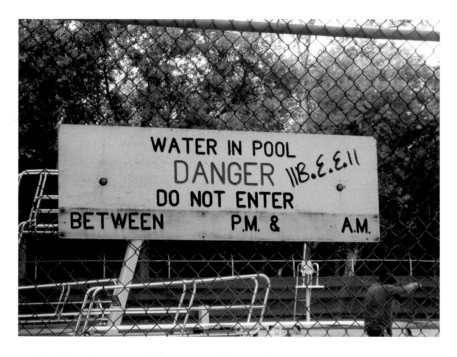

Your hotel may provide a swimming pool.

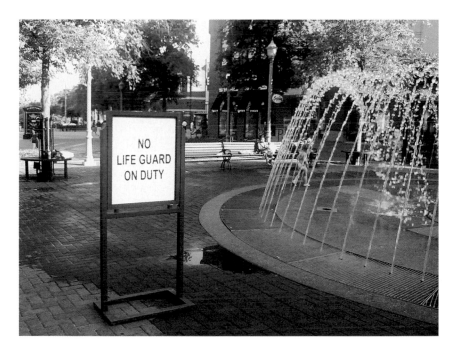

If not, FAIL Nation offers a wide variety of aquatic options. (Use at your own risk.)

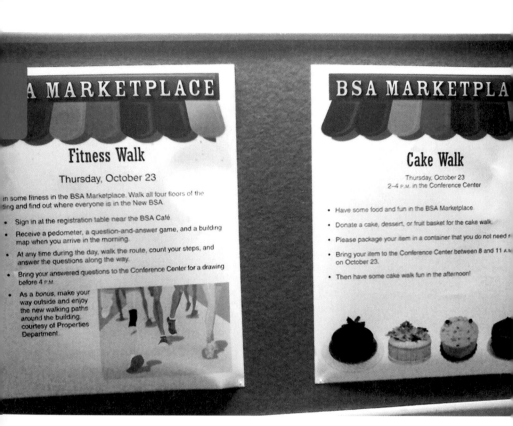

Join the FAIL Nation community by participating in neighborhood events.

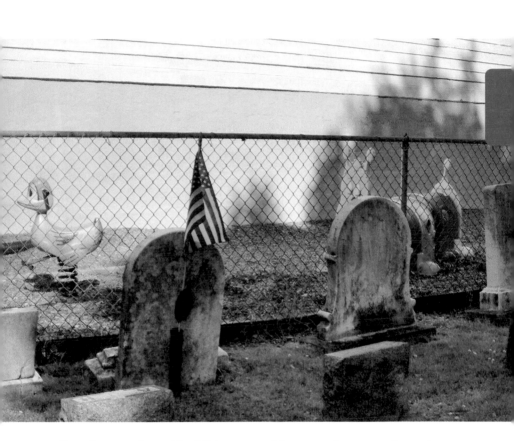

If you're traveling with children, consider spending some time at one of our famed playgrounds. Many also provide resting options for the elderly.

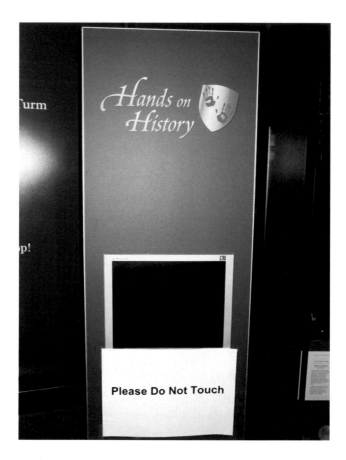

Visit one of our museums to experience some "hands on" activities.

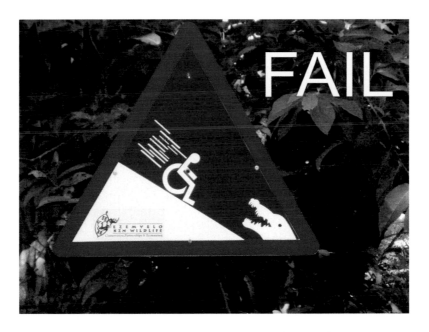

And remember: Even the disabled can experience adventurous and exciting activities in FAIL Nation.

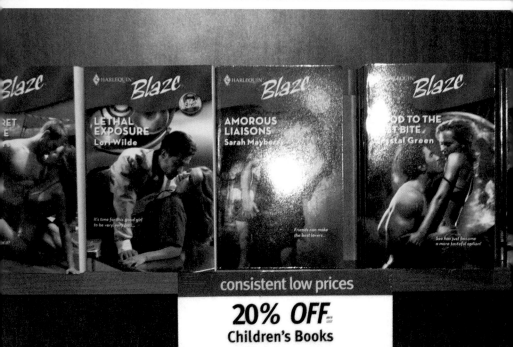

consistent low prices

20% OFF _{MFR LIST}
Children's Books

SHOPPING

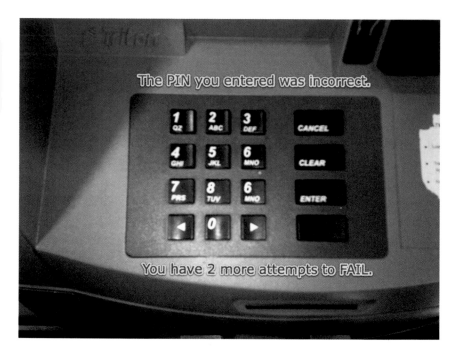

Although most shops take credit cards, the FAIL Nation Bureau of Criminals suggests that you always travel with cash.

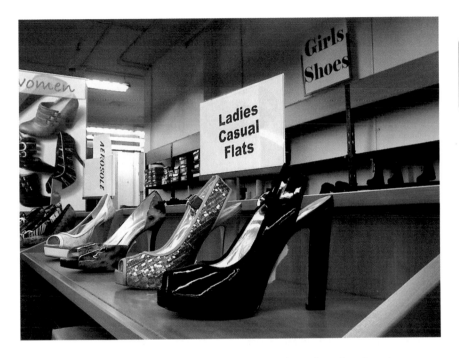

High-end boutiques cater to a new generation of professional women.

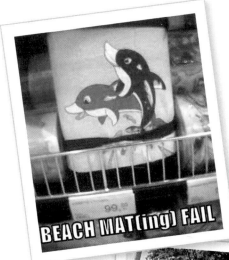

Find whimsical treasures at a FAIL Nation flea market.

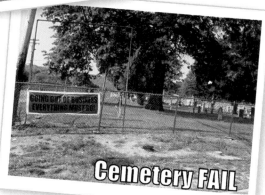

Or consider buying a unique keepsake from an unexpected place.

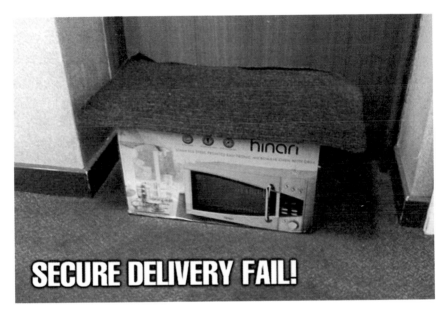

If your items are too heavy to carry, many shops will securely mail them to your hotel free of charge (for a fee of $50).

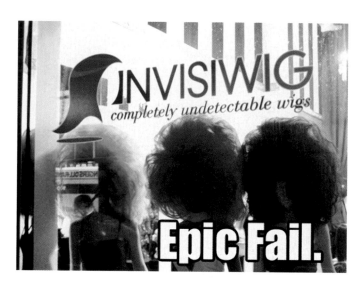

Buy a wig to blend in naturally with the locals.

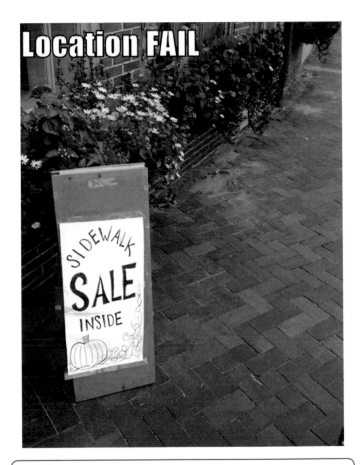

Location FAIL

 ProTip: In FAIL Nation, a sidewalk sale typically occurs inside the store.

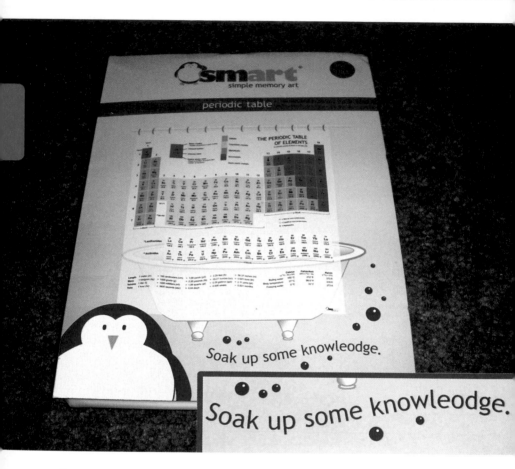

Spruce up your child's bathroom with an educational shower curtain.

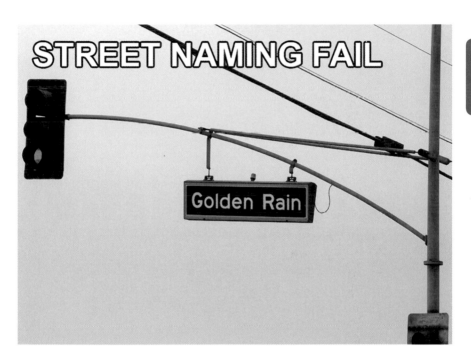

The Golden Rain district offers some of the best shopping for children's items.

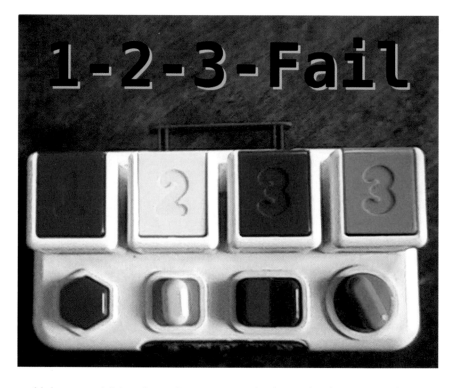

Help your children learn how to count in the native language of FAIL.

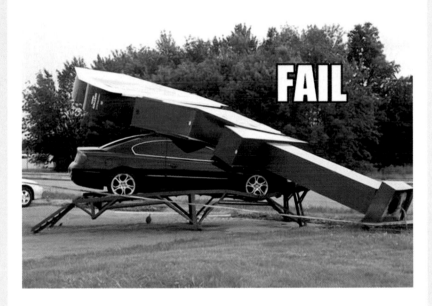

Sometimes buying a slightly used car can be cheaper than renting.

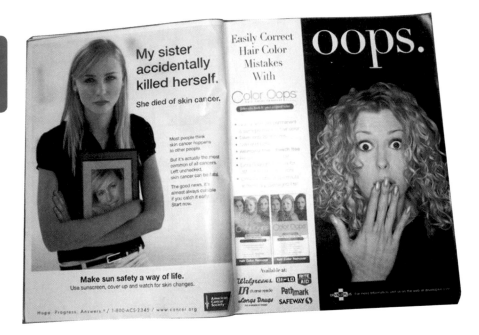

Purchase a magazine for the trip home.

SOUVENIRS

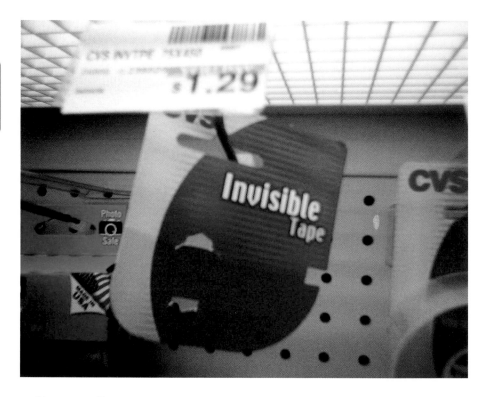

For yourself

Handy for wrapping gifts!!

5 bananas
5
five
MY FIRST FAIL

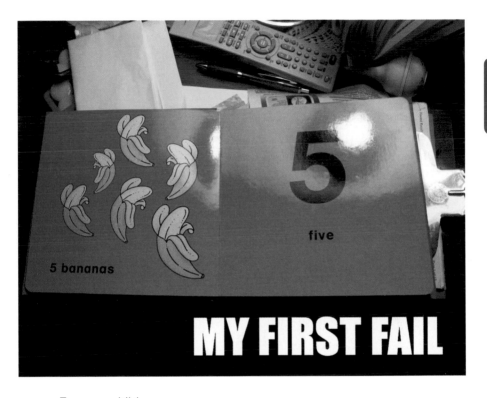

For your child

Herb Day
Lip & Eye
Remover
WATERPROOF
THEFACESHOP
Herb Day
Lip & Eye
Remover
TESTER

For your niece

LA FOLIES DES
TOUGHEST TOYS
ON WHEELS!
STEEL
MADE
Buddy L

For your nephew

Ask how you can adopt this dog
Charities
FAIL
Ask how you can

For your mother

Loss of
Family Member
Congratulations
Congratulations
Sympathy
YOU SUCCEEDED!
FAIL

For your father

LEMONS

Was

110

Lemons

Perfect for orange juice.

WHERE TO EAT

STAYING IN

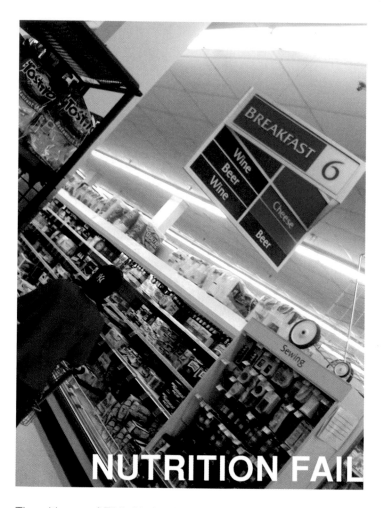

NUTRITION FAIL

The citizens of FAIL Nation know that breakfast is the most important meal of the day.

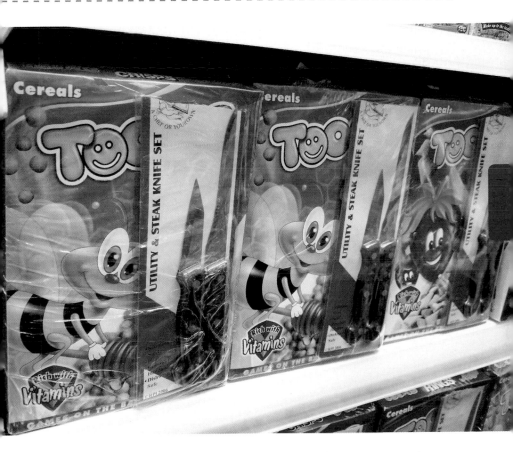

Two items are frequently packaged together for extra convenience.

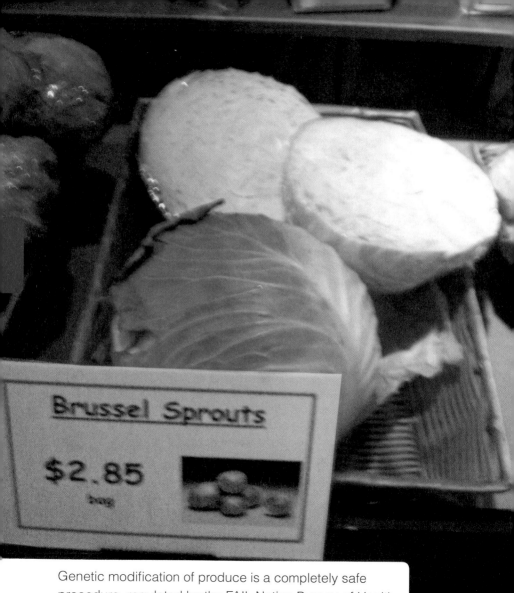

Brussel Sprouts

$2.85
bag

Genetic modification of produce is a completely safe procedure, regulated by the FAIL Nation Bureau of Health.

University of FAIL

Interested in a government career in Health?
Graduate with a degree from our

GENETIC MODIFICATION PROGRAM

in less than 3 weeks!

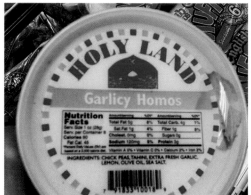

FAIL Nation accepts all sexualities . . .

. . . and has produce and
deli items to meet all
lifestyle needs.

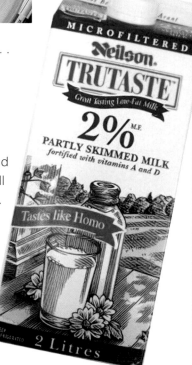

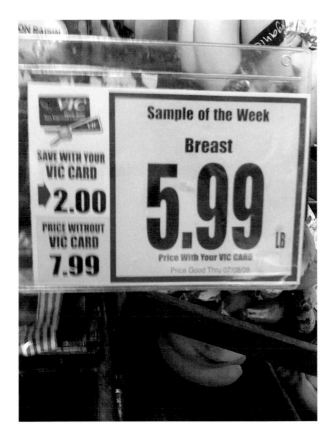

For dinner, live it up! Try an exotic new meat.

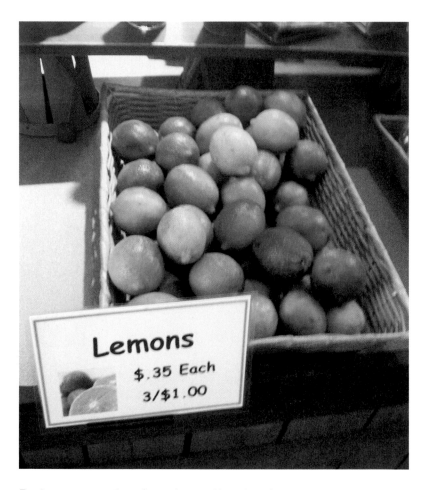

Reduce your carbon footprint and buy local.

Note: All FAIL Nation produce is imported from Peru.

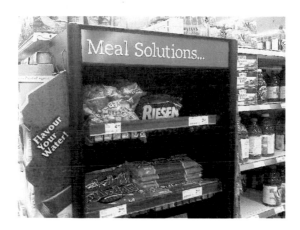

Active lifestyle with no time to shop? Many supermarkets offer quick solutions for healthy eaters.

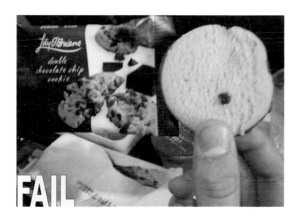

No meal is complete without dessert.

TOWN OF AGAWAM
HEALTH DEPARTMENT

FOOD LICENSE

EXPIRES JUNE 30, 2006

Main Pavillion
Six Flags New England
Agawam, MA

EXPIRES JUNE 30, 2006

PICTURE TAKEN IN
JUNE 2008

Fail

DINING OUT

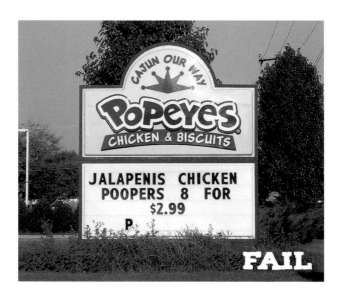

Many restaurants use billboards to showcase
their wit and mastery of puns. An annual billboard
competition is held twice a month in FAIL City.

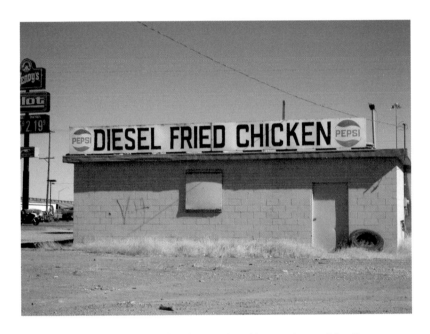

Eating out in FAIL Nation is cheap, healthy, and good for the environment.

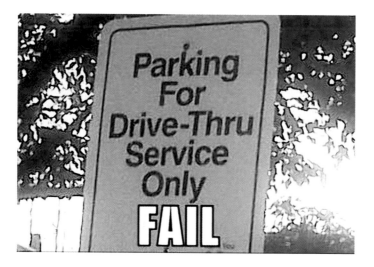

All Diesel Fried Chicken restaurants offer parking for our drive-thru customers.

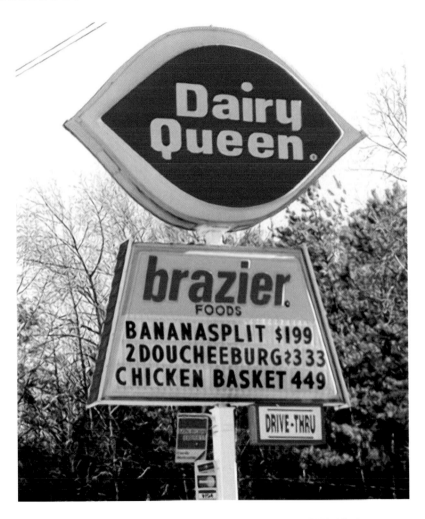

Other familiar drive-thrus may serve new items in FAIL Nation.

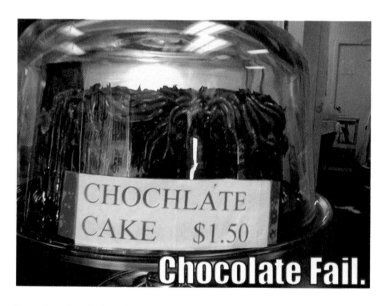

CHOCHLATE CAKE $1.50

Chocolate Fail.

Running late? A cake can make a great snack!

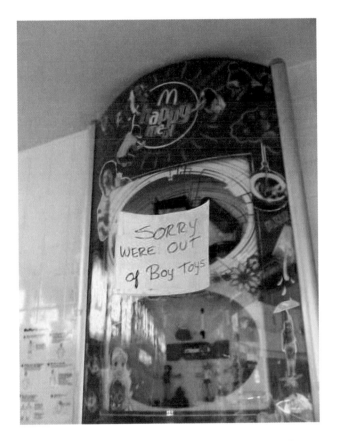

Does your child or cougar have a picky palate?

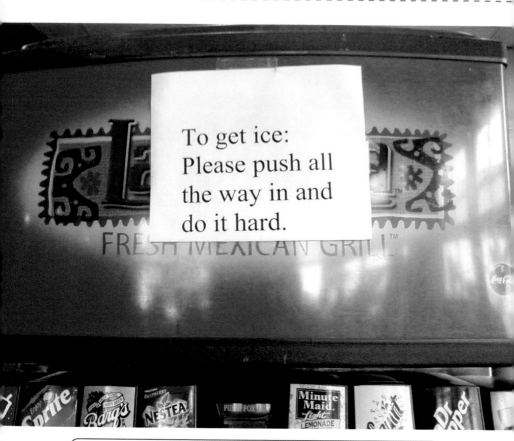

To get ice:
Please push all
the way in and
do it hard.

PRO-TIP **ProTip:** Make sure you do it hard.

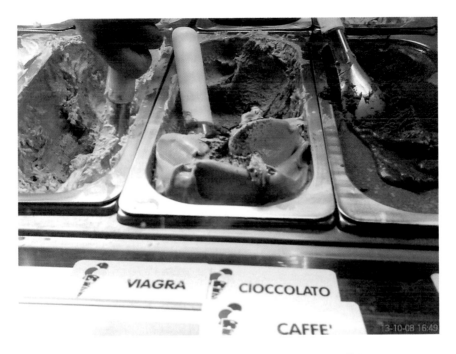

Always save room for dessert! You'll be sure to burn off the calories.

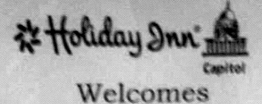

Sexual Harassment

FAIL

WHERE TO STAY

LODGINGS AND AMENITIES

ELECTRIC ROOM

SPRINKLER ROOM

In case of fire, all electric rooms are equipped with state-of-the-art sprinkler systems.

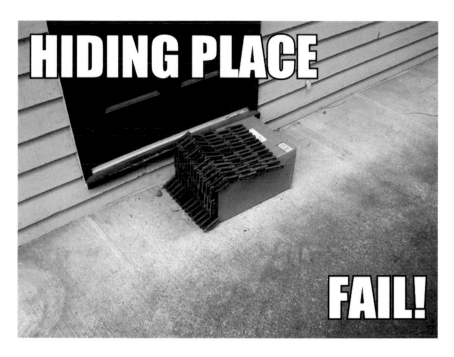

Many hotels and motels provide hiding places for you to store your valuables during your stay.

Hotel Grande

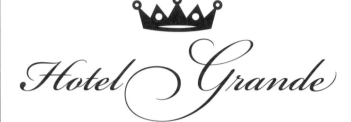

FOR YOUR
CONVENIENCE
AN ELEVATOR
IS LOCATED IN
CHINA

Convenience FAIL

 has conveniently located
elevators for all of our disabled
customers.

Not recomended
Elevator located
very far from room
& goes to Great
Britain

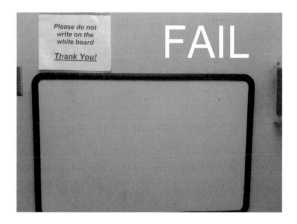

Some motels provide free amenities for business travelers during the off-season (from March 30 to February 12).

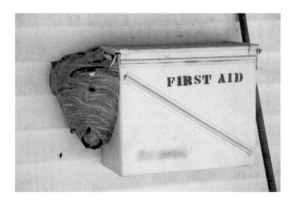

Make sure you test out the first aid kit that comes with your room.

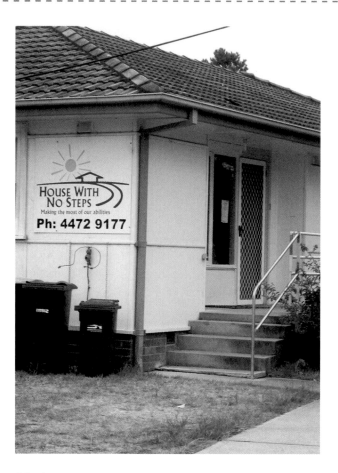

All of our motels are wheelchair friendly.

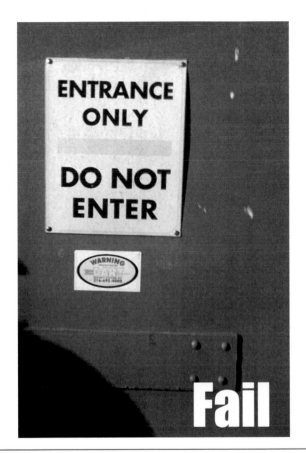

 ProTip: When confused, follow the directions printed in the bigger type.

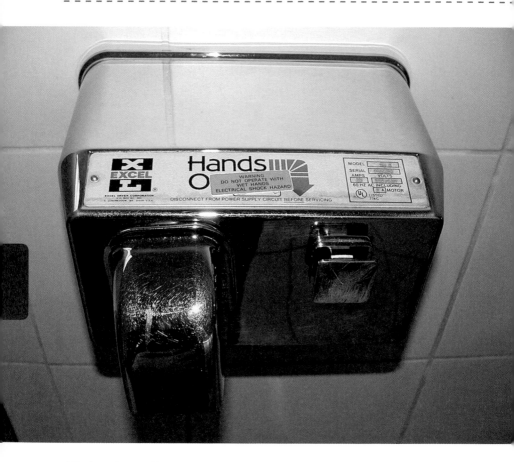

All electric appliances come printed with instructions for ease of use.

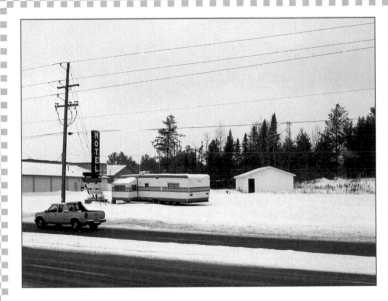

Winter Wonderland Motel

Cozy and quaint motel in a quiet neighborhood with ample parking and easy access to room.

Winter Wonderland awaits your arrival at Motel.

 Expandable rooms available.

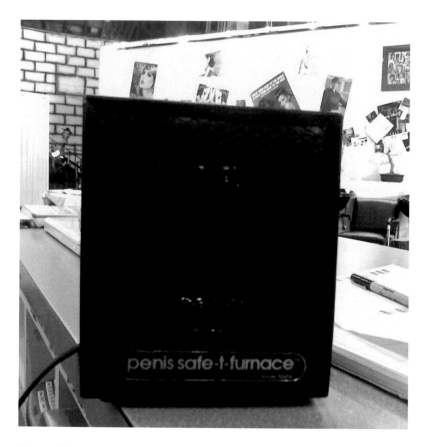

If you did not register for insurance upon arriving in FAIL Nation, check that your hotel or motel has a safety furnace to avoid costly hospital visits.

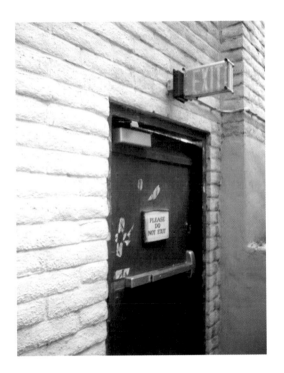

Please do not exit FAIL Nation.

FAIL
Bottomless Pit
65 feet deep

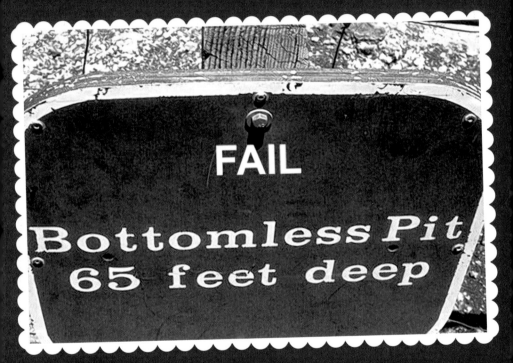

WHAT TO SEE

- - - - - - - - - - - - - -

LANDMARKS AND SIGHTSEEING

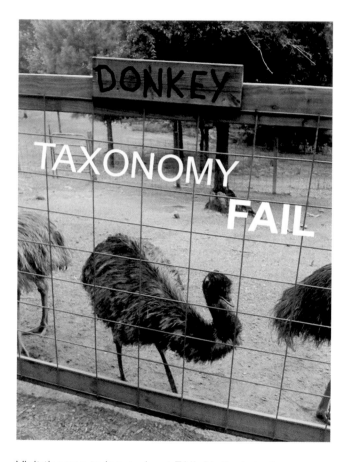

Visit the zoo to learn about FAIL Nation's indigenous animals.

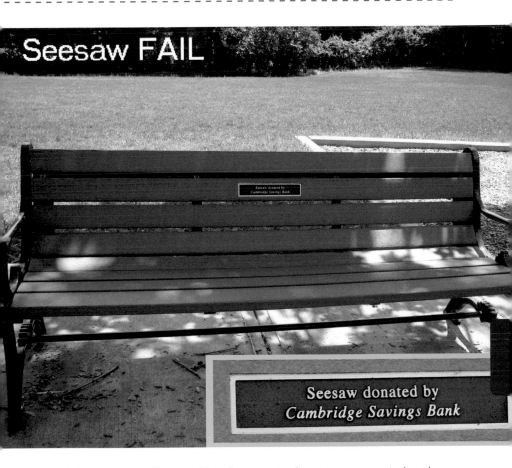

Seesaw FAIL

Seesaw donated by
Cambridge Savings Bank

It is customary for small businesses to donate seesaws to local parks.

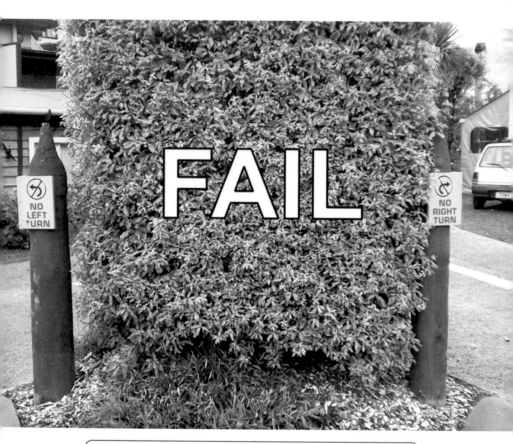

 ProTip: If no signs indicate an exit, look for an elevator (usually located in China).

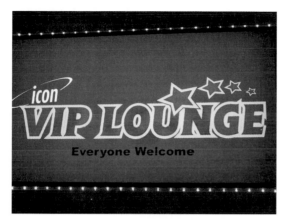

Check out a VIP club to experience the inclusively exclusive FAIL Nation nightlife.

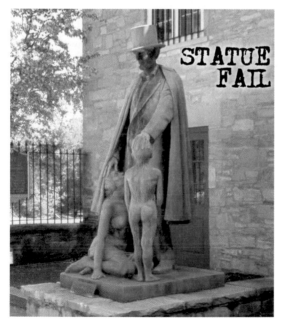

Statues are frequently erected in plazas and town squares.

FREE TRIP TO HEAVEN
DETAILS INSIDE
FAIL
SS 9-30 WORSHIP 10-30

👎👎👎👎👎

TOURIST
ACTIVITIES

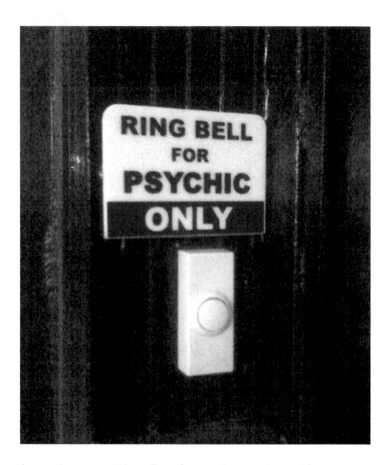

Learn how your trip will go from a licensed psychic.

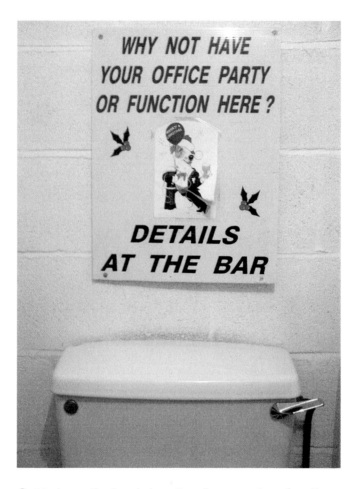

Get to know the locals by attending a party or function.

Baby Party Pacifiers

So good, they're almost addictive!

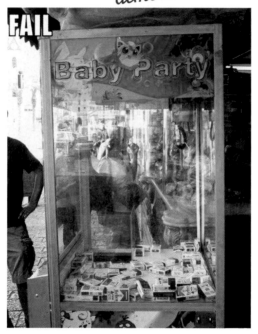

High-quality pacifiers are available from vending machines for those traveling with children.

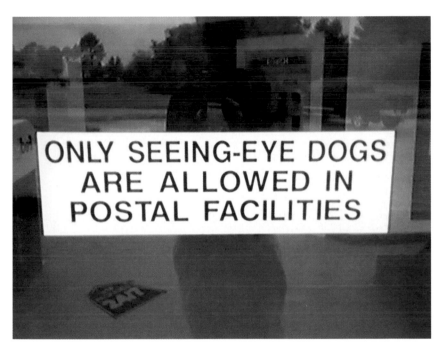

If you need to send a postcard, visit the seeing-eye dogs at the post office. In FAIL Nation, the postal worker bites you!

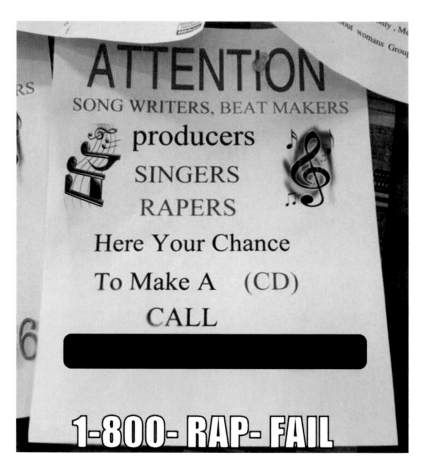

In partnership with the FAIL Nation Bureau of Criminals, all studios permit producers, singers, and rapers to record music free of charge. (A fee of $50 may apply.)

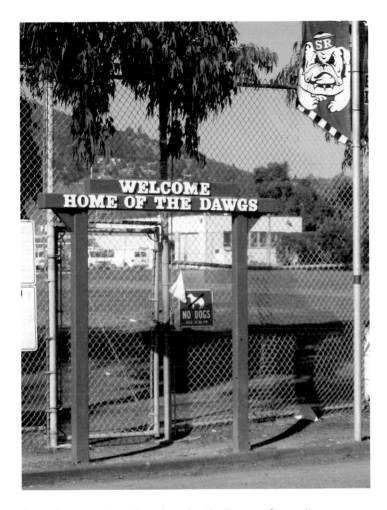

Attend a postal worker–free football game for a cheap afternoon of fun.

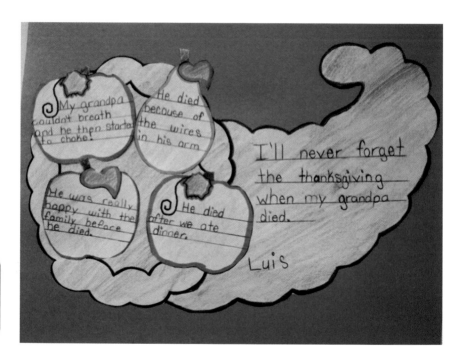

Make sure your children remember their vacation by helping them start a diary.

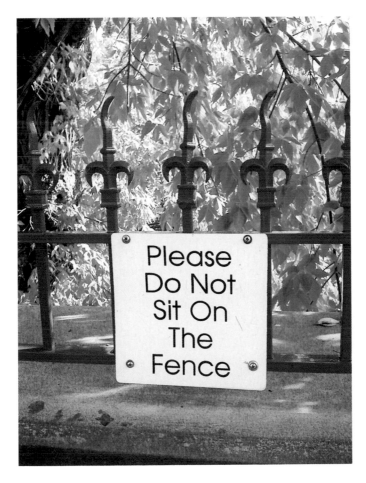

Safcty is a concorn in FAIL Nation. All park fences are clearly marked with warnings, and touching an electric fence is punishable by death.

Estonia Sweden
GSM 050 23094
Fax 046 33027
GSM 070 8929540
Fax 0515 14220
ASS TRANSPORT

TRAVELING WITHIN FAIL NATION

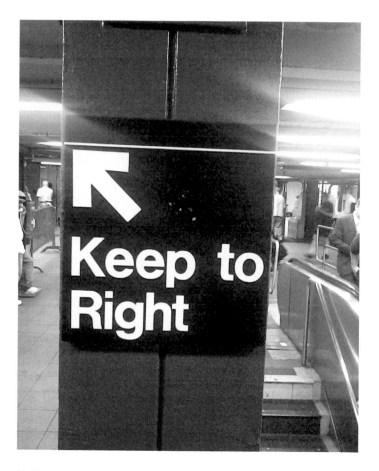

Follow directions when using public transportation.

INTEGRATION FAIL

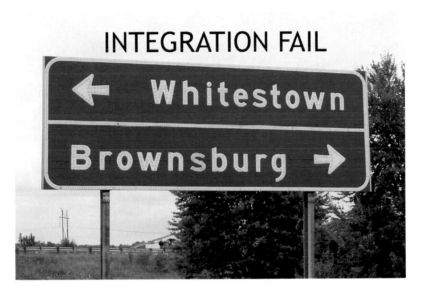

Leave the city and spend a day exploring our colorful suburbs . . .

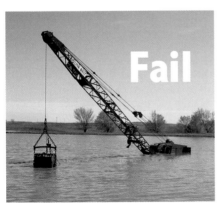

. . . or the countryside.

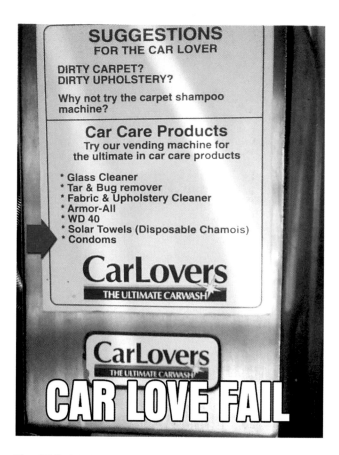

The FAIL Nation Bureau of Transportation encourages safe driving.

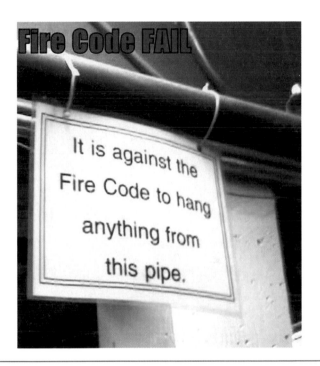

 ProTip: It is against the Fire Code to hang anything from pipes, including those used for smoking.

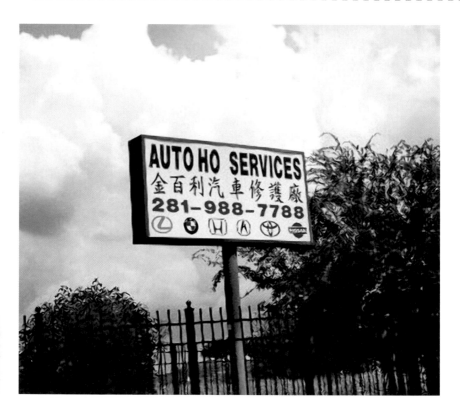

Know where to turn in the likely event of an accident.

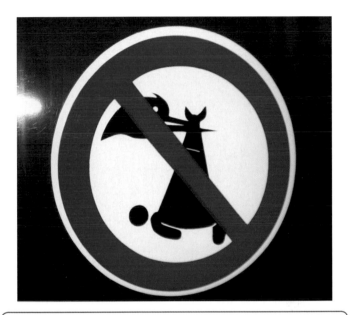

 ProTip: Traveling by stork is illegal in FAIL Nation.

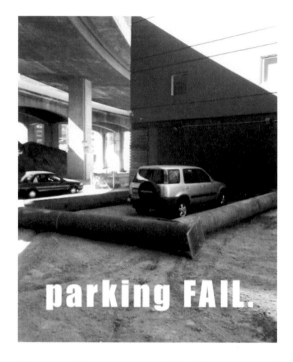

Some parking spots are difficult to get out of.

Let's all take a ride on the

Music City

250

I'M LOST

GRAY LINE
Nashville, Tennessee

FAILBUS

Save money by taking a scenic bus tour instead of driving.

For
150 yds

TRAVELING WITH CHILDREN AND THE HANDICAPPED

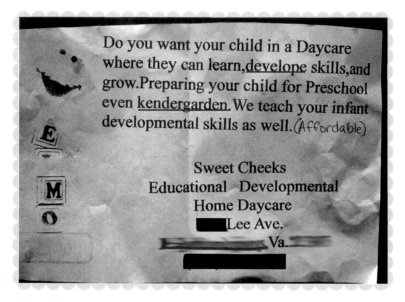

Do you want your child in a Daycare where they can learn,develope skills,and grow.Preparing your child for Preschool even kendergarden.We teach your infant developmental skills as well.(Affordable)

Sweet Cheeks
Educational Developmental
Home Daycare
■■■Lee Ave.
■■■■■■■■Va.

Consider enrolling your children in day care for the duration of your stay.

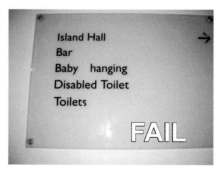

Island Hall →
Bar
Baby   hanging
Disabled Toilet
Toilets

FAIL

For travelers on a budget, baby hanging is a popular alternative to day care.

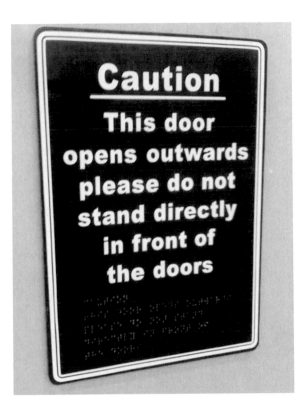

FAIL Nation is braille friendly!

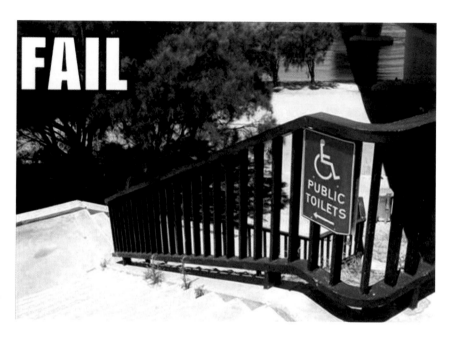

For the safety of wheelchair-bound individuals, all stairways are equipped with handrails.

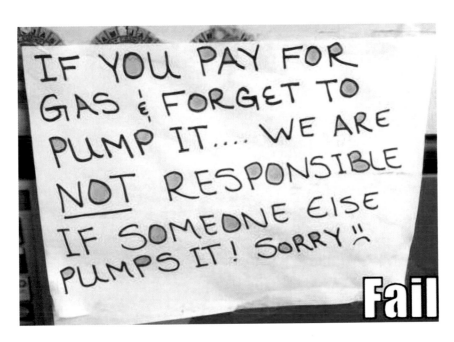

Elderly drivers, beware.

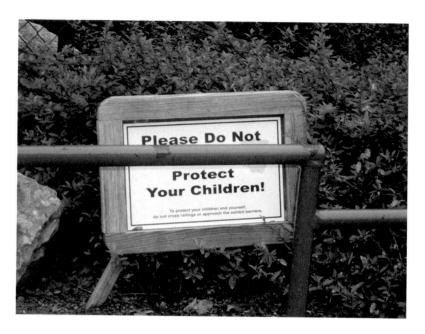

Named for the famous naturalist, "Darwinism" parks are a tourist hotspot in FAIL Nation.

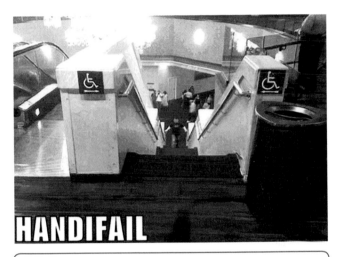

HANDIFAIL

 ProTip: Check handicap ramps prior to use.

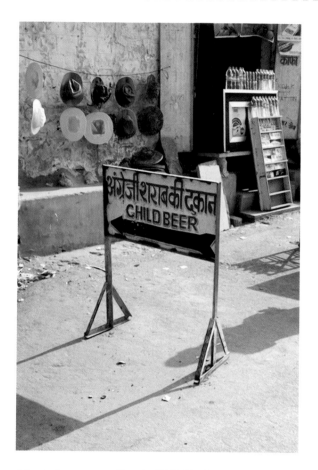

Alcohol consumption in FAIL Nation is limited to
those under 30 to encourage a robust child-per-
capita rate.

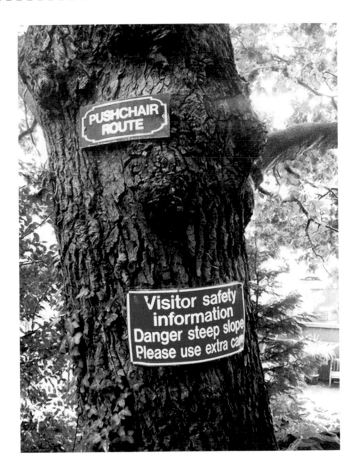

Scenic parks are full of helpful signs to allow the disabled a carefree experience.

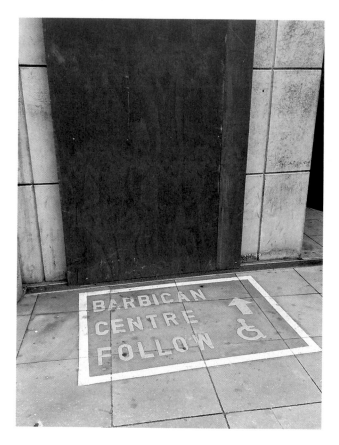

Should you become crippled during your visit to
FAIL Nation, support groups are easily accessible.

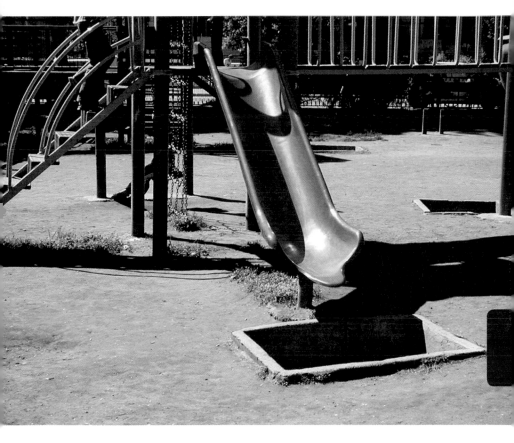

FAIL Nation playgrounds provide endless thrills for the young child.

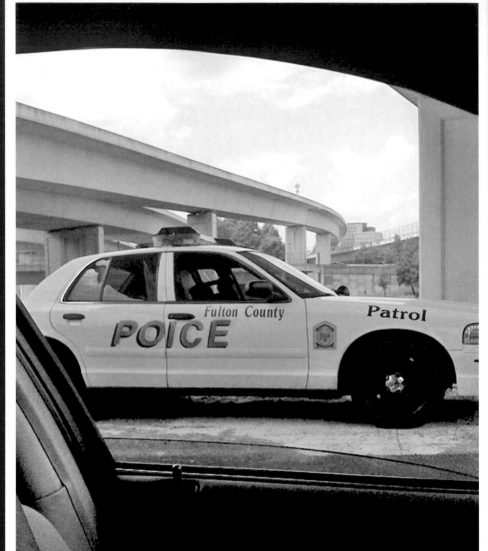

Fulton County

POICE

Patrol

SPELLING FAIL

UNDERSTANDING THE CULTURE

- - - - - - - - - - - - - -

SAFETY

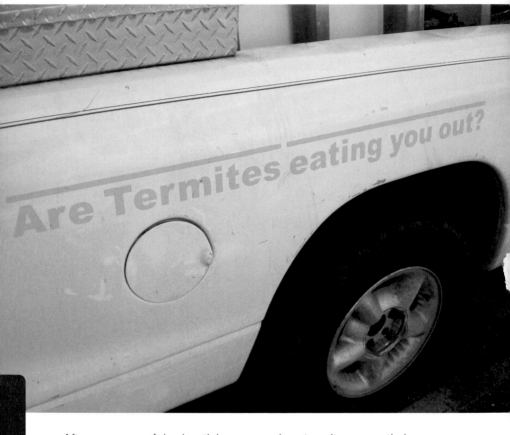

After a successful advertising campaign, termites recently became extinct in FAIL Nation.

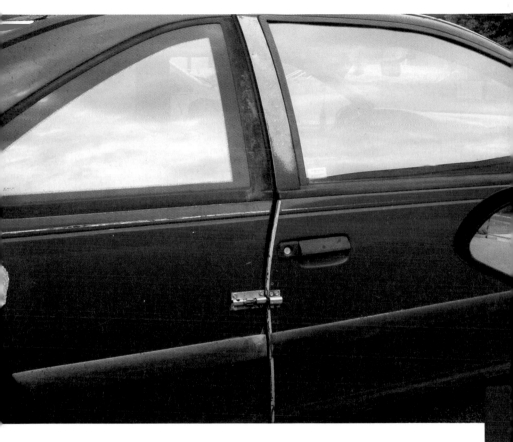

Although FAIL Nation is rated 678th in the world for safety, many citizens still choose to add extra protection to their homes and cars.

BREAK GLASS
FOR HAMMER

USE HAMMER TO
BREAK GLASS

FAIL

All buses are equipped with hammers to be used in the event of an emergency.

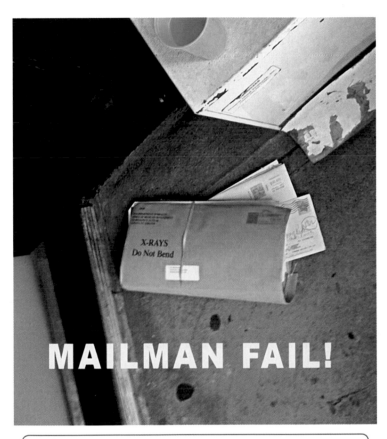

MAILMAN FAIL!

ProTip: X-rays actually *do* bend.

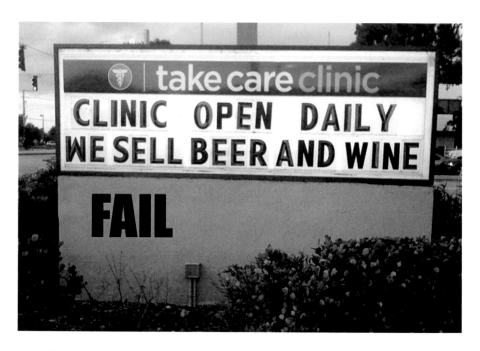

The medicinal use of alcohol is a safe homeopathic remedy for most common aches and pains.

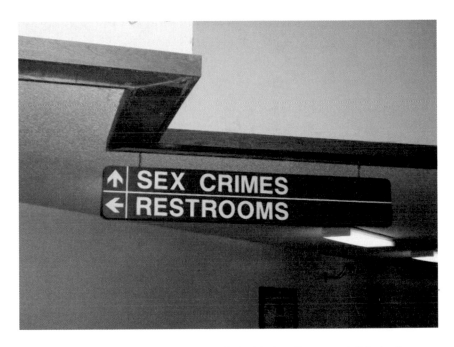

Thanks to extensive work by the FAIL Nation Bureau of Criminals, it is now illegal for crimes to be conducted outside of specially marked crime areas.

10
Black Velvet Cape
Spanish
FAIL

DIPLOMATIC
RELATIONS

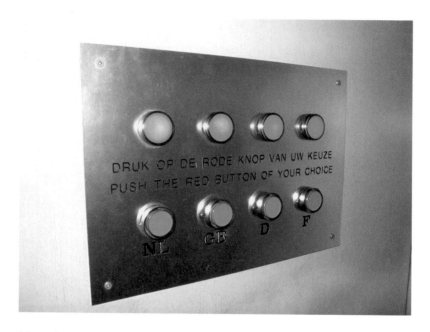

Many hotels offer elevator service to the Netherlands, Great Britain, Denmark, and France.

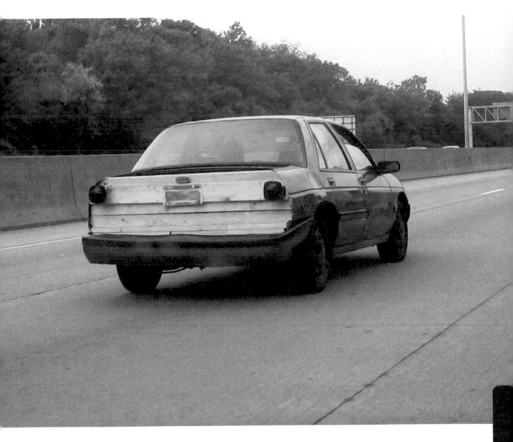

Custom car parts are the primary export of FAIL Nation.

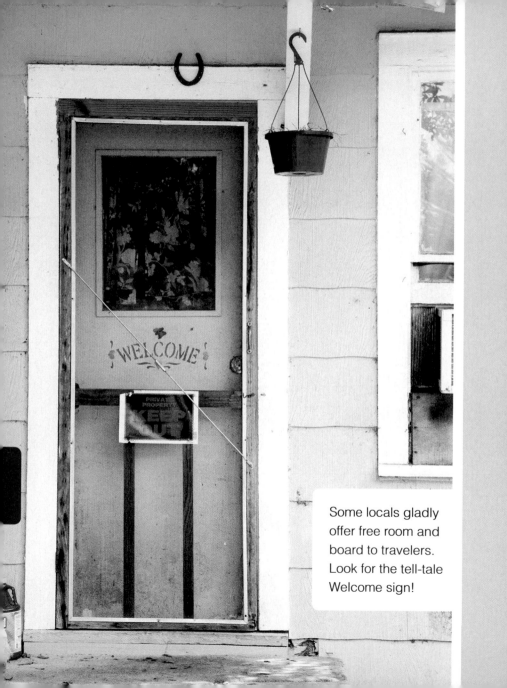

Some locals gladly offer free room and board to travelers. Look for the tell-tale Welcome sign!

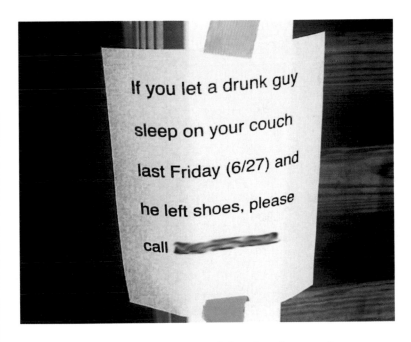

Letting a native sleep on *your* couch in return is a great opportunity to make friends.

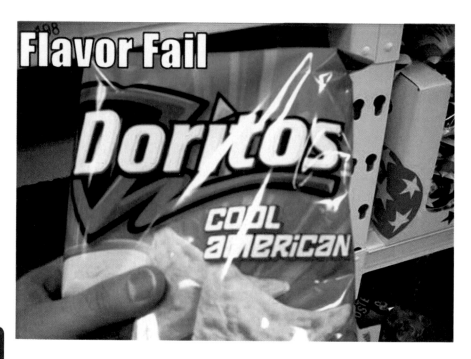

The citizens of FAIL Nation are particularly fond of American culture.

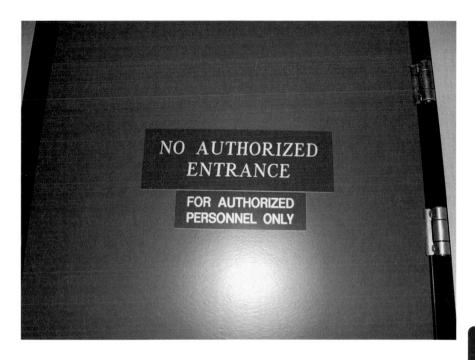

To speed up customs, FAIL Nation has separate entrances for authorized personnel. Not for use by authorized personnel from 8 a.m. to 12 a.m.

STAY OFF
THE GRASS

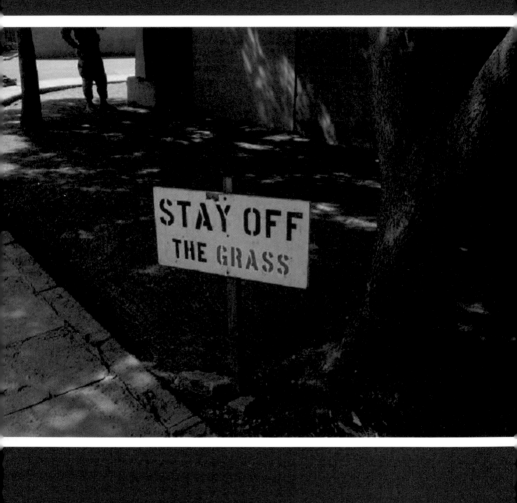

GREEN NATION

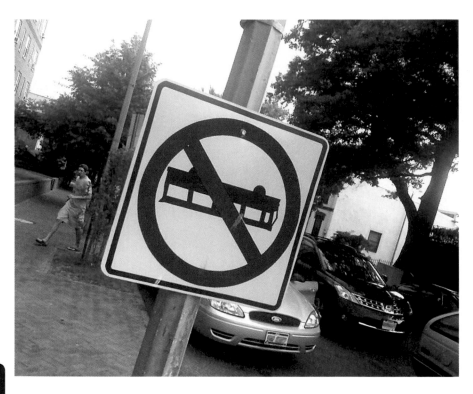

After an extensive study, buses that travel upside-down were abandoned for the more efficient right-side-up buses.

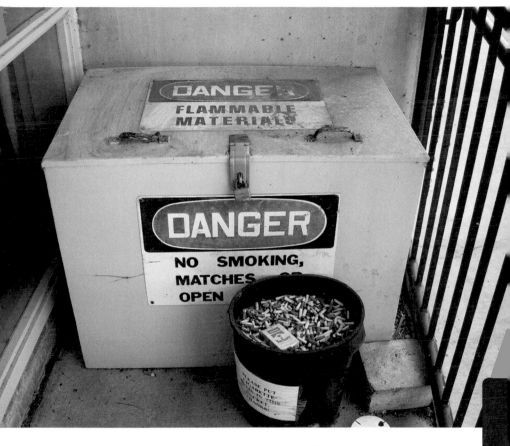

To discourage smoking, smoking areas are frequently located by flammable materials or toxic waste.

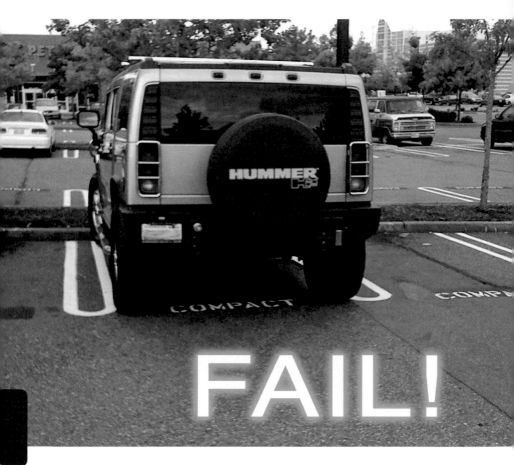

Many FAILers choose to drive compact cars to reduce their carbon footprint.

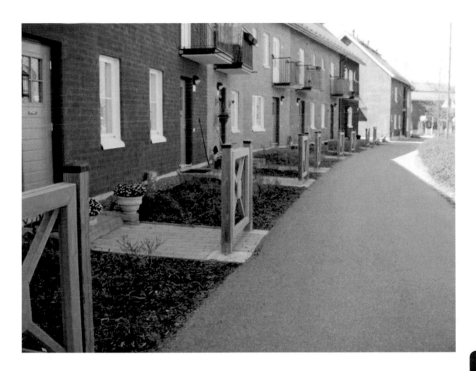

Houses are often built with invisible fences so that fewer trees are used.

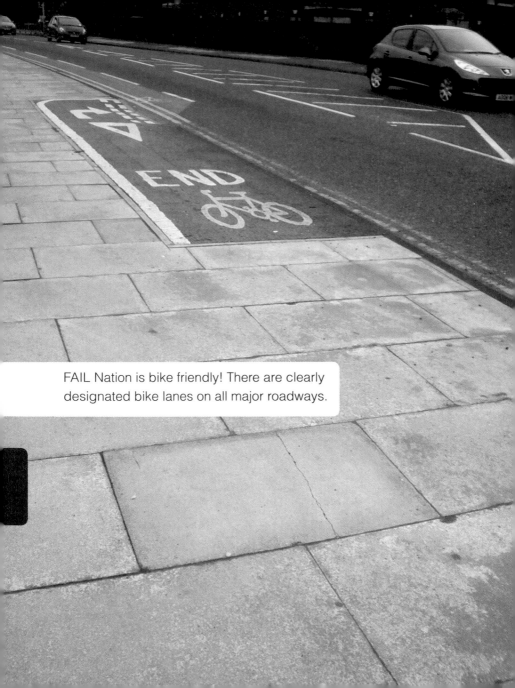

FAIL Nation is bike friendly! There are clearly designated bike lanes on all major roadways.

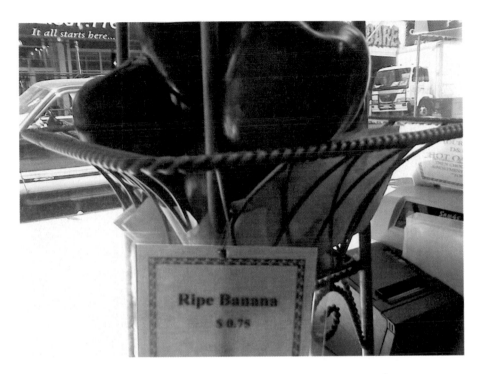

Despite accusations that all FAIL Nation produce is imported from Peru, local farmers encourage citizens to keep buying fresh fruit.

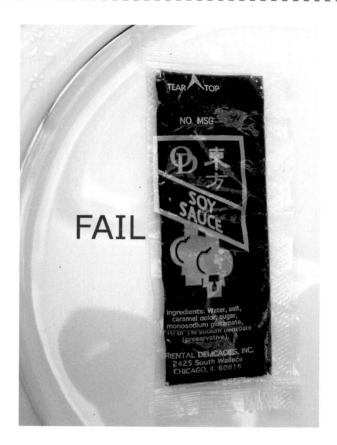

Food is never made with chemicals, preservatives, or MSG.

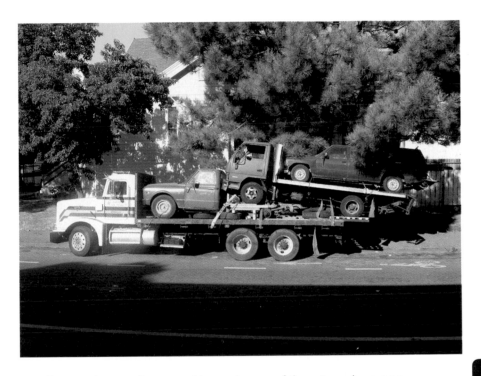

Tow trucks are dispensed in packages of three to reduce gas usage.

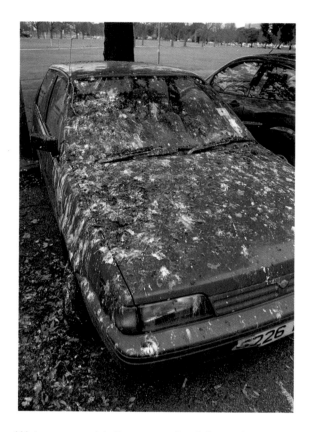

Water-use restrictions must be followed.

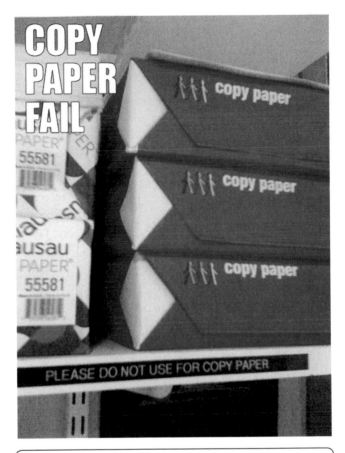

COPY PAPER FAIL

copy paper

copy paper

copy paper

PLEASE DO NOT USE FOR COPY PAPER

ProTip: Conserve paper by not using copy paper for copies.

COMARO CHRONICLE
September 17, 2008
SOUTHERN SUBURBS - SOUTH
GOOD NEWS
Numbers 6:24-26:
satanism is REAL

SPIRITUALITY

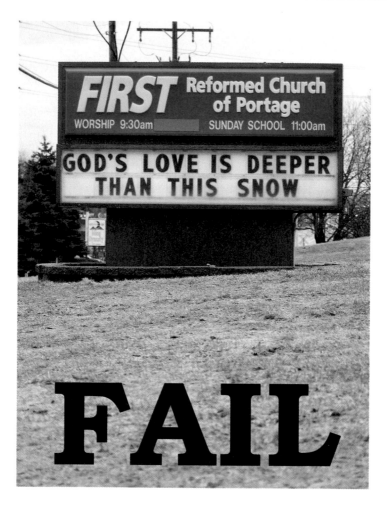

. . . But not as deep as the Bottomless Pit.

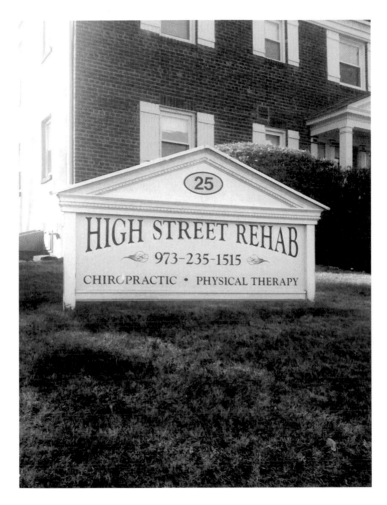

Many FAIL Nation twelve-step programs offer additional steps for no extra cost. (A fee of $35 may apply).

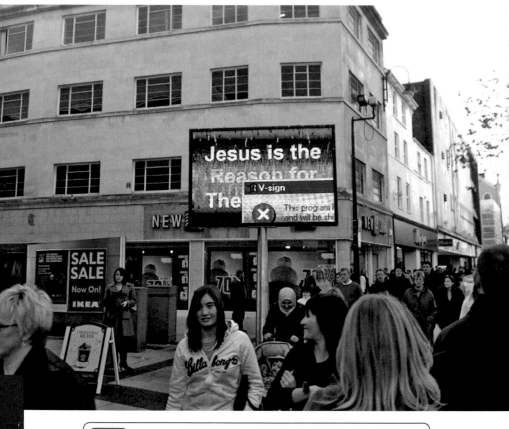

PRO-TIP

ProTip: You can shift all your blame to Jesus and feel completely free.

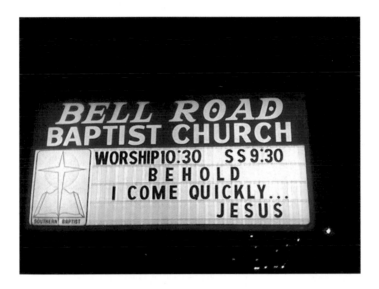

The churches of FAIL Nation combine historic teachings with a modern way of reading scripture.

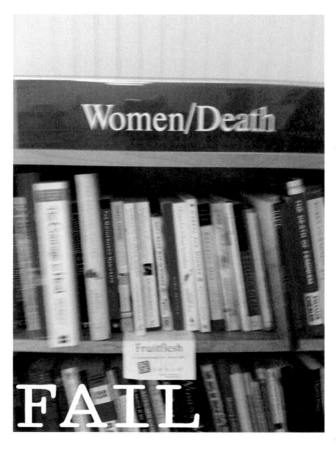

Women especially can benefit from a spiritual awakening in FAIL Nation.

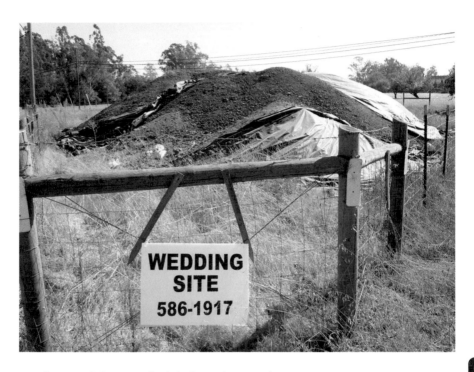

Some might even find their soul mates here.

U-FAIL
U-HAUL

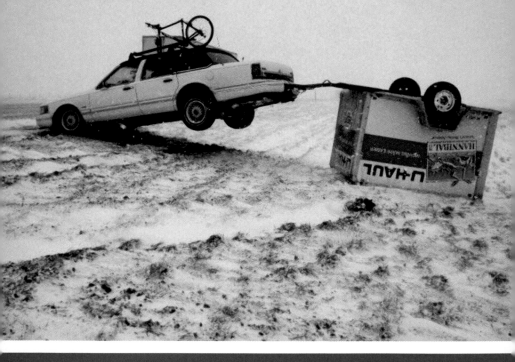

MOVING TO FAIL NATION

- - - - - - - - - - - - -

Yes   No

Do you have any experience with vocal percussion (aka beat boxing)?

Yes   No

If not, would you be willing to learn?

Yes   No

Do you have any experience raping?

Yes   No

If yes or no, which rapper would you most like to be and why?

_____

_____

What other major commitments do you think you might have this year

_____

_____

 ProTip: FAIL Nation does not accept work visa applications during the tourist season, which lasts from the end of March to mid-February.

Literacy is important, so make sure you have the necessary skills before immigrating.

COLLEGE OF SANDWICH ARTISTRY

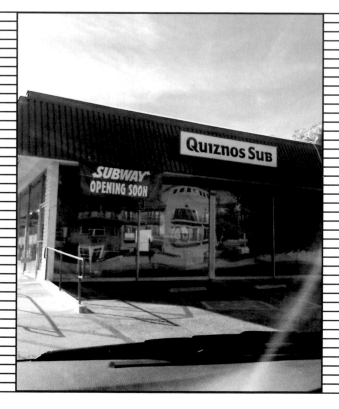

Getting a job without a degree is hard. But a graduate from the College of Sandwich Artistry has plenty of job opportunities!

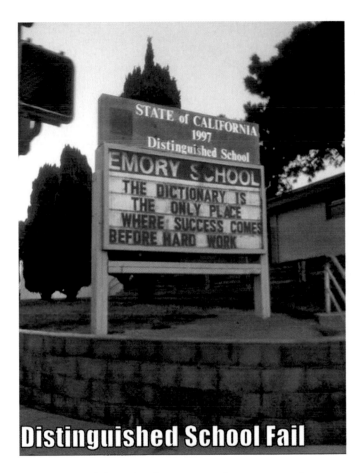

Choose the right school to ensure the success of your children.

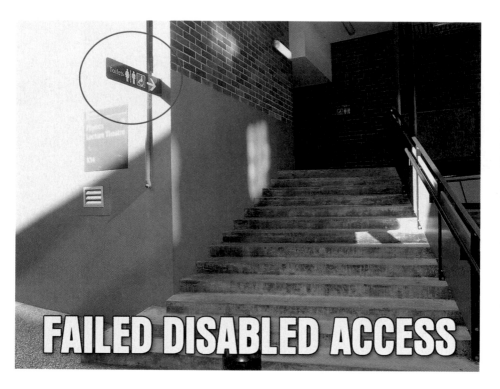

If your children have special needs, why not send them to a boarding school that can meet those needs?

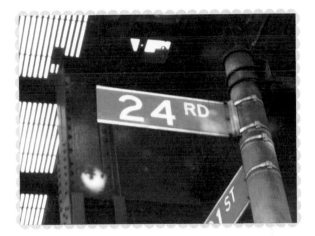

Many immigrants choose to live in the
neighborhood surrounding 24rd Street.

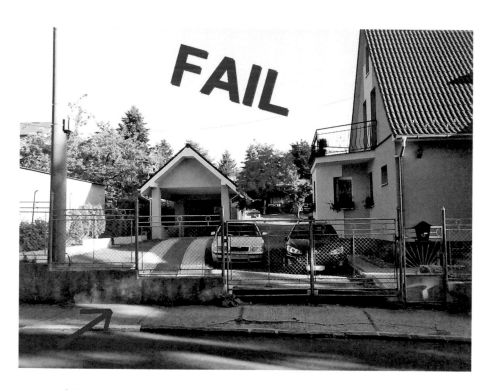

Welcome to your new home!

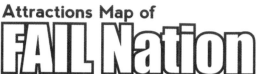

Attractions Map of
FAIL Nation

National Population: Over 9,000
Capital: Fail City
Time Zone: FST
Area: Slightly less than 5 times the
size of Quebec.

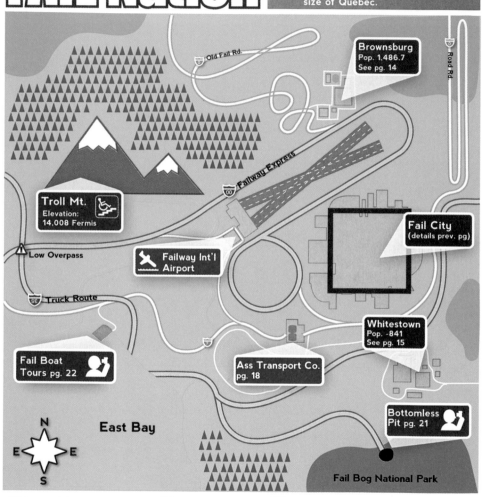

Old Fail Rd.

Brownsburg
Pop. 1,486.7
See pg. 14

Road Rd.

Failway Express

Troll Mt.
Elevation:
14,008 Fermis

Fail City
(details prev. pg)

Low Overpass

**Failway Int'l
Airport**

Truck Route

Whitestown
Pop. -841
See pg. 15

**Fail Boat
Tours pg. 22**

Ass Transport Co.
pg. 18

**Bottomless
Pit pg. 21**

N
E   E
S

East Bay

Fail Bog National Park

■ National Attractions   ■ National Parks   ■ Government & Business
■ Cities & Villages   ▲▲▲ Public Landfill

Explore Appetizing
Fail City

Metro Population: Over 9,000
Area: About 4,000 Sq. Furlongs
Zip Code: 31337
Area Code: 911

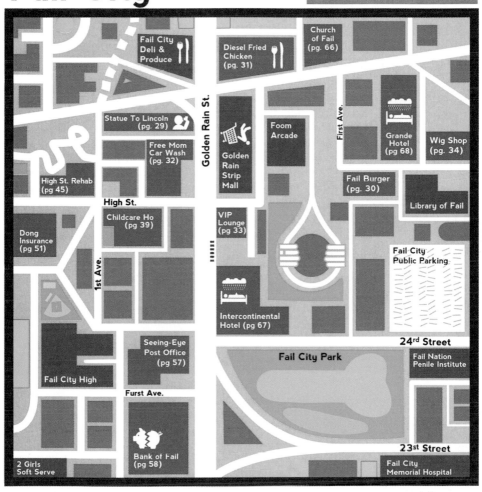

Street Map Legend

◼ Pro Tip Locations   ◼ Places of Interest   ◼ Public Park   ‖‖‖ Bike Lane

$\{\}$ $\{\}$ $\{\}$ $\{\}$ $\{\}$

CONTRIBUTORS

LISTED IN ORDER OF APPEARANCE

Entrance not an entrance—Kimberly Zenz (Hi, Seanathan!)
Misspelled dictionary—Dane Coleman
Maximum amount $250.00—David Crosta
Stock market fortune cookie—Gordon Good
Diseases—Alex Applegate
Use an action verb—Jordan Schulman
Dong insurance—Ginger Williams
Who is the general manager?—Adam Bell
FAIL car—John Pelton
Treat dad to a 3way—Christopher Winters
Childcare/Ho—Gidget
Sexuality ends here—Ron T. Blechner
Tree protection area—Jesse DeGraff
Helicopter rides—Cindy Proulx
Live lobsters—Eileen and Jenna Gartland
Hitler perfume—Ian Hurley
Free cunt breakfast—Cameron Liner
Need the remote—Photo by Bobby James, submitted by Todd Oblak
Cheeseburger w/o girls—Daniel Beyra
Sponge windshield wiper—Dwayne La Rose
12 hour parking—Milo Hyson
Guest speaker on drugs—Joe Tian and Sean Zheng
Free mom—Greg May
Select asses—Darrell Claunch
Still eating kids for free—Ian Lowe
Four urinals—Thomas Curwen
Free food hunger banquet—Kyle Beamsderfer
DIY car side mirror—Mike Deere
Biker about to fall—Mike Deere
Bumper fail—Jason and Julie Malmberg
Drive thur—Aaron Lewis
Water in pool—Lindsay Greschuk and Jonathan Viel
No life guard on duty—Emily Burns
Fitness and cake—anonymous
Playground next to cemetery—Tamara Szafranski and Jerry Pollack
Hands on history—Nico Pesci
Wheelchairs and alligators—Kenneth Riper
Children's books—Meghan Zimmer

Misnumbered ATM—Andrew Tetlaw
Ladies casual flats—Candy Ellison
Beach mat(ing)—p&d
Going out of business—Mandy Hoskins
Secure delivery fail—Heckie Cormack
Completely undotectable wigs—Eric Singleton
Sidewalk sale—Vincent Busam
Soak up some knowleodge—Liz Halpin
Golden Rain street—Colleen O'Rourke
1-2-3-Fail—Andrew Fry
Car dealership mishap—Sara Marschand
Oops—Kaydee Blinn and blinnks.com
Invisible tape—Bert McMahan
My first fail—Dan and Kathleen S.
Lip & eye remover—Erika Poole
Toughest toys on wheels—Richard Dupuis
Adopt this dog—Brandon Wertz
You succeeded!—Alexander Dorokhine
Perfect for orange juice—Ashley Carnes
Nutrition fail—Paul Goodman and pdgoodman.com
Cereal and knife packaging—Tom Nixon
Brussel sprouts—Kelly Gondek
Garlicy homos—Heidi Ocel
Tastes like homo—Geoff Bardwell
Sample of the week—Keeley Carrigan and blooempire.com
Lemons—Kelly Gondek
Meal solutions—Marc Snelgrove
Double chocolate chip cookie—Sam Sutton
Expired food license—Zev Eisenberg
Jalapenis chicken poopers—Birkey/Schrader
Diesel fried chicken—Hafeeza Jaffer
Parking for drive-thru—Ethan Linkner
Doucheeburg—Ginger Williams
Chochlate cake—Trent and Bonnie Walton and Robert Feuille
Out of buy toys—Photo by John Lindley, submitted by Katie English
Push all the way in and do it hard—Kristen Paulsen
Viagra ice cream—Karel Sirks
Holiday Inn welcomes sexual harassment—Kevin and Joseph Lamour

CONTRIBUTORS

Electric room/Sprinkler room—Joe Cicman
Hiding place fail—Koriann Brousseau
For your convenience—Mikael T Daugherty
Please do not write on the white board—Scott Morlin
First aid—Anonymous
House with no steps—Megan Canny
Entrance only, do not enter—Ronald Pasko
Do not operate with wet hands—Cameron Rogers
Fail motel—Adam Sinason
Penis safe-t-furnace—Kris Hickman
Please do not exit—Kimberly Zenz (Hi, Seanathan!)
Bottomless pit—Vinakro (Vincent Ha)
Taxonomy fail—John C. Watkins V
Seesaw—Jessi Champion
No turning—Andrew Maclean
VIP lounge—Will Ross
Suggestive statue—David A. Miclette
Free trip to heaven—Collin Waters
Ring bell for psychic—Neal Groothuis
Details at the bar—Liz Andrews
Baby party—Rachel Weisshaar and Jonathan Pulvers
Seeing-eye dogs—Ben Allen
Attention rapers—Craig and Robin Bartlett
No dogs allowed—Graham Charles
The Thanksgiving when my grandpa died—Andy and Jane Deitrich
Do not sit on the fence—Dave Wilson
Ass transport—Khyber Courchesne
Keep to right—Marcin Olkowicz
Whitestown and Brownsburg—Seth Gitter
Failblog countryside—Tammy Sharp
Car love—Winston Yang
Fire code—Scott and Ariana Morrow
Auto ho services—Ginger Williams
No flying by stork—David Neves
Barricaded parking—Brendan Finlayson
I'm lost—Rebecca Huntemann
For 150 yds—Nicholas Edmonds
Sweet cheeks daycare—Jen Meade
Baby hanging—Stuart Gibson
Caution—Colin Taylor
Public toilets—Chris Buckley
We are not responsible—Schmitty and randomlynothing.com
Do not protect your children—Melissa DePlanche
Handifail—Phil Westcott

Childbeer—Mark Levesley
Pushchair route—Ryan Niven
Barbican centre follow—Thomas Curwen
Playground slide—Glen Richter
Poice car—John C. Watkins V
Are termites eating you out?—Michael Clements
DIY car lock—Ash and Clay B.
Break glass for hammer—James Millington
X-rays do not bend—Rafal Samplawski
We sell beer and wine—Justin Visca
Sex crimes and restrooms—Chico DeGallo
Spanish translation—Michael Jones
Red button of your choice—Richard Dupuis
Wooden car repair—Paul Zuest Jr.
Welcome—Christy Brown and seabel.com
He left shoes—Andrew Benton
Cool American—Steve McNaughton
For authorized personnel only—guLin
Stay off the grass—Jonah Munsell
No upside-down buses—John S. Mitchell Jr.
Danger—Charles Bryant
Compact Hummer—Thaddeus Moore
Gate with no fence—Thaddeus Moore
Bike lane—Sarah Smith
Ripe bananas—Ben Therrien
No MSG—Mary Beth
Tow truck cubed—Justin Berthelsen and Mark Schick
Dirty car—Mike Deere
Do not use for copy paper—Michael Simoneau
Good news—M
Deeper than this snow—Drew Everett
High street rehab—Mark Willner
Jesus is the reason—Richard Jones
I come quickly—Daniel and Rachel Mills
Women/Death—Andy Warren
Wedding site—Melia Dicker
U-fail—Luke Stay
Do you have any experience raping?—Nate Seymour
We support the library's—J. E. Harper
Subway opening soon—Alexander Brown
Success before hard work—Jonathan McKay
Failed disabled access—Winston Yang
24rd street—Christine Vales and Zachary Collinger
Unusable driveway—Jakub Urban